# DOGS
# IN THE
# AIR

This edition first published in Great Britain in 2015 by Orion
an imprint of the Orion Publishing Group Ltd
Carmelite House
50 Victoria Embankment
London EC4Y 0DZ

3 5 7 9 10 8 6 4 2

A CIP catalogue record for this book is available from the British Library.

Hardback ISBN: 978 1 4091 6071 7

Designed by Smith & Gilmour
Edited by Emma Smith

Picture credits: David White / REX: page 119; Getty: page 9, 10, 14, 20. 28-29, 45, 108, 109; Image
Broker / REX: page 98, 107, 120-121; iStock: page 24, 25, 27, 32, 34-35, 42-43, 44, 46, 49, 52-53, 54, 58,
60, 62-63, 64-65, 72, 76-77, 91, 100-101, 118; PA Images: page 13, 15, 16-17, 114; James Smith: page 122;
Mirrorpix / Arthur Sidley: page 19; William Hartley: page 12, 18, 22, 26, 33, 40, 48, 66, 87, 104, 112-113.
All other images: Shutterstock.

Printed in the United States of America

The Orion Publishing Group's policy is to use papers that are natural, renewable and recyclable
and made from wood grown in sustainable forests. The logging and manufacturing processes
are expected to conform to the environmental regulations of the country of origin.

Every effort has been made to fulfil requirements with regard to reproducing copyright material.
The author and publisher will be glad to rectify any omissions at the earliest opportunity.

www.orionbooks.co.uk

ABOUT THE AUTHOR

Jack Bradley is from the
Peak District and enjoys long
walks over the hills, wild
swimming and cozy nights
in by the fireside. Jack lives
at home with his family.

*Legs outstretched, eyes focused and ears flapping: a dog in the air is a spectacular sight.*

This book is a celebration of that simple pleasure: dogs bounding through fields, over fences and playing catch, full of energy and jumping for sheer joy. With contributions from around the world, this astounding compendium of photographs has the power to surprise, delight and uplift. From a Jack Russell Terrier on a beach in Oregon, to a Hungarian Puli in Germany and a Cockapoodle on Hampstead Heath in London, this is a truly heart-warming and inspiring collection of man's best friend in motion.

Some are majestic, some steely with determination, some are wild-eyed and some are positively gleeful. Whatever the expression, and whether they are elegant or awkward, these images capture those fleeting wonderful moments and the love we feel for our canine companions.

Following on from *Dogs Hanging Out of Windows* and with over ninety-five incredible portraits, this book showcases top pet photography from around the world that will take your breath away. Guaranteed to raise a smile, I hope that this beautiful anthology of dogs in the air will bring you as much happiness as it has for me.

*Jack Bradley*

**Havanese.** Native to Cuba, these fluffy and affectionate dogs can jump hay bales surprisingly well.

[OPPOSITE]
**Dachshund.** These dogs are a miracle of proportions and, as H.L. Mencken once said, they are 'a half-a-dog high and a dog-and-a-half long'. This airborne puppy flies through the air in Manchester, UK.

**Yorkshire Terrier.** A happy Yorkie bounds over a meadow. This breed was originally developed to catch mice and rats in the mills and mines of Northern England so they're full of bravado and have an energetic spirit.

**Springer Spaniel.** Living up to their name, these dogs love springing around. This is Olly jumping high in the Lake District, UK.

**Shih Tzu.** Raphael jumps a hurdle during an agility competition on the second day of the Reliant Park World Series of Dog Shows, in Houston, USA.

**Jack Russell Terrier.** A warmly dressed jumping jack making shapes on Hobbit Beach, Oregon Coast.

[OPPOSITE]
**Hungarian Puli.** Fee making a spectacular mop-like sight as she clears an obstacle at a dog show in Dortmund, Germany.

**Cocker Spaniel.** Lilli, the four-month-old gundog, leaps over the grass. These dogs are known for their ever-wagging tail and eager-to-please temperaments.

**Dachshund.** Ernie the long-haired Dachshund launching himself into the air in a London park.

[OPPOSITE]
**English Cocker Spaniel.** The name Cocker comes from their original purpose – hunting woodcock in England. They are excellent retrievers, affectionate pets and are known to be too friendly to strangers to be an effective guard dog!

**Pug.** First brought to Europe in the 16th century by the East India Company, Pugs have a stern appearance but a warm and cheerful character.

[OPPOSITE]
**Great Dane.** Impressive in size and gait, these dogs need plenty of exercise and lots of room to play. This is Huxley in the early morning sunlight in east London.

**Labrador Cross.** Leaping among the leaves, Conker the Labrador Cross enjoys an autumnal walk in Alexandra Park, London.

**American Staffordshire Terrier.** Staffies love their people and their playtime. This one has gained impressive height chasing a Frisbee up a tree.

**Mixed Breed.** A dog jumps
a hurdle in an agility course.

**Dogo Canario.** Originating from the Canary Islands, these were first bred as fighting dogs in the early 19th century. They are strong and powerful so require experienced and dedicated owners.

[OPPOSITE]
**Labradoodle.** A cross-breed first developed for allergy sufferers, these playful and intelligent dogs are now becoming increasingly popular in their own right. This is Rosie.

**Jack Russell Terrier.** Flying high. These terriers were bred by the Reverend John Russell, a parson and hunting enthusiast, who wanted a dog with high stamina and the tenacity to chase out foxes from the ground. They can jump surprisingly high for a small dog.

**Schnauzer.** Catching the sunlight in a cold Norwegian autumn. With their bushy eyebrows and bristly beards, Schnauzers are an aristocratic and dignified breed who make wonderful family pets.

**Labrador Retriever.** A yellow Lab dives from a pier, heading for a summer swim. With their sunny disposition and sense of fun, you can always rely on this breed to make a splash.

**Chinese Crested.** These dogs suffer the stereotype of being ugly, with contrasting plumes of long hair against their hairless skin. Yet they are very social and devoted creatures. Unlike many other dogs, they have almost no urge to go outside – so this is a rare view of one bounding over the grass.

**Springer Spaniel.** With a pink coat to keep fur at least a little bit clean, Coco jumps to get a better view of Lake Windermere in the Lake District.

**Danish-Swedish Farmdogs.** Always eager to play, these dogs were historically used on farms in Denmark and Sweden. They do have a tendency to chase small animals (and tennis balls).

**American Staffordshire Terrier.**
An incredible expression from
a fun-loving prankster dog.

**American Pit Bull Terrier.** Ready for lift off. This breed need an experienced handler as they have strong personalities with the muscle to match. They were originally brought to the USA by Irish immigrants in the 19th century.

**West Highland White Terrier.** Big ego for a small dog, the 'Westie' has boundless energy. This wee whitey gains some height jumping on the beach.

**Black Labrador.** Delta the black lab rises majestically over the misty valleys beneath Gummer's How in Cumbria.

[OPPOSITE]
**Catalan Sheepdog.** With its weatherproof coat blowing in the breeze, this hardy dog breed is often a flock-herder or a guard. A Catalan Sheepdog also played the part of Einstein in the *Back to the Future* film.

**Cocker Spaniel** going for the ultimate belly flop. The breed was developed to work in dense undergrowth – but this one is clearly happy to try diving into a swimming pool.

**Bassett Hound** with jowls a-jiggling as he gathers pace on the snow. These dogs might be floppy-eared, sad-looking and droopy but they are highly intelligent and brilliant trackers.

**Border Collie** playing happily in the snow. This lively and tireless breed is known for its low boredom threshold and high intelligence.

**Bull Terriers** in perfect unison, probably before their synchronized swim. They might look intimidating, but with the right owner they can be good-natured pets.

[OPPOSITE]
**Springer Spaniel** flying over the snow. This breed have been around a long time – spaniels were reportedly mentioned in Welsh law over 1700 years ago!

**Cockerpoo,** Lara, suspended in mid-air.
This breed is a cross between a Toy or
Miniature Poodle and a Cocker Spaniel.

**Siberian Huskies** are very resistant to the cold, as the indigenous people of eastern Siberia have long used them as sled dogs. Here are two burning off extra energy in the snow-laden woodland.

**American Staffordshire Terrier** poised perfectly in the air. More heavily built than its English counterpart, these 'Staffies' are still bold and loyal companions.

**Dalmatian.** Made popular by a Disney film, these were originally used as 'carriage dogs' to trot alongside horse-drawn vehicles. This one is a gallant galloper in the early evening sun.

Border Collie enjoying a game of Frisbee in the park. Blue-eyed collies are often said to have glass eyes or 'watch' eyes.

**Jack Russell Terrier.** Amazingly fast and agile, this dog certainly has a spring in its step.

**Golden Retriever.** First bred in Scottish Highlands by Sir Dudley Marjoribanks (also known as Lord Tweedmouth), these dogs have an incredible sense of smell and are often used as guide dogs, sniffer dogs and water rescue dogs.

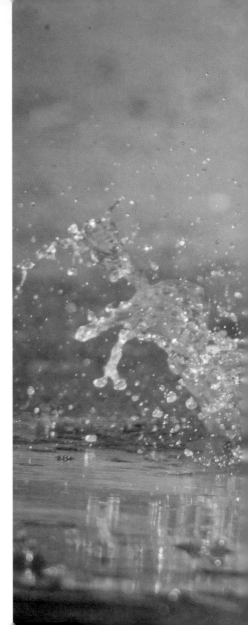

**Dachshund** looking determined as he careers towards the water. This wire-haired dog makes a loyal and inquisitive companion.

[OPPOSITE]

**Chihuahua.** These fun-loving, fun-sized dogs are the smallest dog breed in the world but are full of personality. They came to prominence in the Mexican state of Chihuahua in the 1890s, hence their name.

**Giant Schnauzer.** Standing tall, the Schnauzer is bold and valiant. Often stoic and seemingly serious, Schnauzers have a mischievous and playful streak.

**Tibetan Terrier.** Originally companions to the nomadic herdsman wandering the high plains of Tibet, this breed was first raised by monks in lamaseries (monasteries presided over by a llama). They were thought to bring good fortune so were nicknamed as Luck Bringers or Holy Dogs and were only ever given as gifts, never sold.

**Poodle.** Prancing in the powdery snow, this poodle sports a classic styled coat. This grooming used to have a practical purpose – the breed were originally water retrievers and the trimmed areas lightened the weight and wouldn't snag, while long hair around the joints and vital organs protected the dog from the cold water.

**Mixed Breed.** Legs sprawling and stick in mouth, this dog enjoys the beach high life in Spain.

**Samoyed.** Hailing from the nomadic Samoyede people of Siberia, these dogs are tough outdoor workers but also love human companionship. This is Murphy jumping logs in Hampstead Heath, London.

**Yorkshire Terrier**. A puppy doing his best Superman pose on the beach.

**Irish Setter.** Known as the 'red dog' or 'Modder Rhu', this fiery breed have a zest for life and love to play.

**Yorkshire Terrier.** Picking up the pace. Yorkies are vivacious characters with a tenacious spirit; they might be yappy but they are devoted.

**Coton de Tulear**. Cuddly, cottony-coated and clownish, these dogs love to fool around. Here's one looking rather serious, jumping clear over a log.

**Beagle,** chasing down the camera. These scenthounds are happy-go-lucky animals with a love of running off the lead and a strong instinct for following a trail.

**Italian Corso Dog.** Just hanging out.
Corsos are powerful and graceful creatures.
They need firm guidance and are highly
family-orientated dogs.

**Hungarian Vizsla** jumping gracefully into an urban lake. These big beasts were once hunting dogs in Europe but nowadays they are content to be house dogs – as long as they get plenty of exercise.

**Border Collie.** Collies love to play fetch and catch – this red-coloured one is no exception.

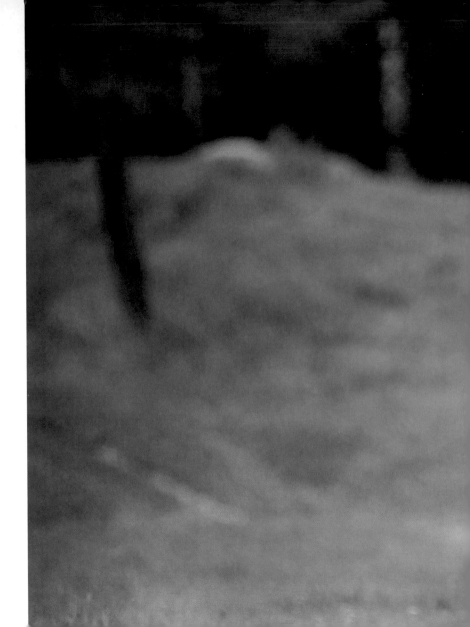

**Rhodesian Ridgeback.** From lion-hunting in Africa to leaping around the local park, these dogs with a distinctive ridge of hair along their spine have come a long way.

**Poodle.** Young poodles like this puppy romp and jump about with great vigour so owners have to be prepared to deal with a lot of bounciness.

[OPPOSITE]
**American Pit Bull Terrier.** These solidly built dogs are characterized by their strength, confidence and enthusiasm. They were first bred to bait bulls and bears but were then put into pits to fight other animals, hence the moniker. This breed is banned in the UK due to the risk of aggression.

[RIGHT]
**Jack Russell Terrier.** Like this little one chasing a ball, Jack Russells need a lot of exercising and a good social life to prevent them becoming snappy and yappy.

**Welsh Springer Spaniel** caught mid-jump. These working dogs have a cheerful temperament and enjoy wandering off – so owners must be on their guard!

**Dachshund.** 'I'm all ears.' A big jump for a little sausage.

**Boston Terrier.** Nicknamed 'the American Gentleman' for its debonair tuxedo-like coat and docile nature, these dogs make affectionate companions.

[OPPOSITE]

**Weimaraner.** Nicknamed the 'grey ghost', Weims have a dignified gait and striking looks. They need owners who can match them in stamina.

**Dachshund.** It's a lot of effort for little legs to get off the ground. This is DD reaching for the skies.

**Spaniel Cross** flying through a spring meadow filled with buttercups. Any dog with a bit of Spaniel in them is almost guaranteed to be curious, quick-footed and a lot of fun.

**French Bulldog** looking surprised at its own height gain. This compact breed like to show off and have a great sense of fun.

**Yorkshire Terrier** hovering above the icy ground. Yorkies usually hate the cold so this one is probably running inside as fast as he can!

**Rough Collie.** A breed made famous starring in the hit TV show *Lassie*, these gloriously coated dogs have a lion-like majesty when jumping through the air.

[OPPOSITE]
**Beagle.** Difficult to resist with their big dark brown eyes and soft expression, beagles are very food-focused hounds. This puppy is practicing for running with the big guys.

**Schnauzer Cross** prancing across the beach. Purebreed Schnauzers are lively, agile and affectionate so any dog with some of their genes are likely to be the same.

**Cavalier King Charles Spaniel.**
Aristocratic-looking, well behaved and
gentle, these dogs have long been a
favourite of royalty.

**German Shepherd.** Also known as the Alsatian, these dogs were originally a protector and herder of sheep. They are responsive to training and often serve as guard dogs and police dogs all over the world.

**Lhasa Apso**. A flying fur-ball in Germany.
This breed were originally watchdogs for
temples in Tibet.

**American Staffordshire Terrier** smiling at the camera before making a splash.

**Havanese** with eyes on the prize, chasing after a toy. These dogs are known as Habaneros in their native Cuba.

**Poodle.** Elvis Presley was a big fan of
poodles – his was named Champagne.
He also gave poodles to all the women
he loved, including his mother.

**Afghan Hound.** Gracefulness personified.
These dogs are elegant and sophisticated but
can sometimes seem aloof. An Afghan Hound
can jump seven feet from a standing position.

**Border Terrier.** This highly popular breed is energetic and cooperative. This is Connie launching herself from a fallen tree.

[OPPOSITE]
**Dachshund** running up the garden path. These dogs are short on leg but big on character. Don't underestimate their toughness – they were bred to take on badgers. ('Dachs' meaning 'badger', 'hund' meaning 'dog'.)

[OPPOSITE]
**Bulldog.** They may look grumpy, but beneath their wrinkles is a lovable companion. They are strong, tenacious and determined – often used as a symbol of courage.

[RIGHT]
**Newfoundland.** These large bear-like dogs were originally used to pull in fishermen's nets. They like to swim and they need space to roam the great outdoors.

**Jack Russell Terrier.** Leaping around in Arkansas, USA, this bouncy and bold terrier enjoys playing ball.

[OPPOSITE]
**Yorkshire Terrier.** These feisty and loyal little dogs have all the confidence expected of a breed several times its size. Here's one happy to be outside jumping around.

**Papillon.** Also known as the Continental Toy Spaniel, these dogs have striking 'butterfly-wing' ears and were a favourite of Marie Antoinette.

**Labrador Retriever.** Ziggy the yellow Lab takes a running jump among the trees. This amiable breed love sport and long daily walks.

**Bearded Collie** competes as a 'super dog'
at the Royal Winter Fair in Toronto, Canada.

**Spaniel Cross** caught in the air. Cross-breeds are believed to be more intelligent than pedigree dogs but there is no actual evidence for this. However, they are at lower risk of some inherited diseases.

**Border Collie.** These dogs are among the most agile and are able to jump very well. This one demonstrates a perfect leg tuck high in the sky.

**Jack Russell Terrier.**
This wire-haired terrier
is a bundle of energy
on the beach.

**Bergamasco.** This breed is hard to make
head-nor-tail of. It was originally bred
for a tough life in the Italian mountains.

**Mixed Breed** running across a harvested corn field, ears flapping and body extended. Brandenburg, Germany.

**Border Collie.** Focused, making a leap towards his precious stick in mid-air, this is Jack on Burbage South Edge, near Sheffield, UK.

**St. Bernard.** These giants of the dog world are almost unmatched in size. They have a lovely temperament but aren't the most popular pets due to the space they take up and the quantities of food they consume!

**Maltese.** The lighter way to enjoy dogs.
These ancient canines are fun-loving,
fearless and friendly.

**Springer Spaniel** in full
flight across the moorland.

**Miniature Pinscher.** These were bred to be farmyard rat-hunters – they are quick, lively and high-stepping.

Chihuahua training for an agility contest.
Curious, bold and alert, they are often
among the top ten recommended watchdogs.

**Plott Hound.** This brindled hunting dog magnificently stretches out before diving into the water. They are mostly used to hunt raccoon, but can go after larger creatures such as coyote and wild boar. Originally the Plott Hound was bred in the 18th century by the Plott family in the Smokey Mountains.

[OPPOSITE]
**Dobermann.** The more activity the better with these dogs; they combine speed with intelligence and good looks.

[RIGHT]
**American Staffordshire Terrier** striking a pose. The Staffie is boisterous, robust and, sometimes, a big show-off.

**Dogue de Bordeaux.** Wonderfully wrinkled and big-headed, the French DDB is self-assured and surprisingly athletic – as demonstrated by this one playing in the sand.

**Goldendoodle**. One of the newest 'designer dogs', these are a lovely mix of the Poodle and the Golden Retriever.

**Border Terrier.** These high-octane little dogs can really jump. Always pepped up and willing to amuse, Borders are guaranteed crowd-pleasers.

**Dalmatian and Beagle.** A spotty dog with
his puppy pal, ready to take on the world!

# INDEX

PAGE 9
Havanese

PAGE 13
Shih Tzu

PAGE 18
Dachshund

PAGE 22
Labrador Cross

PAGE 26
Labradoodle

PAGE 10
Dachshund

PAGE 14
Jack Russell Terrier

PAGE 19
English Cocker
Spaniel

PAGE 23
American
Staffordshire Terrier

PAGE 27
Jack Russell Terrier

PAGE 11
Yorkshire Terrier

PAGE 15
Hungarian Puli

PAGE 20
Pug

PAGE 24
Mixed Breed

PAGES 28-29
Schnauzer

PAGE 12
Springer Spaniel

PAGES 16-17
Cocker Spaniel

PAGE 21
Great Dane

PAGE 25
Dogo Canario

PAGES 30-31
Labrador Retriever

PAGE 32
Chinese Crested

PAGE 37
American Pit Bull
Terrier

PAGES 42-43
Cocker Spaniel

PAGE 47
Bull Terriers

PAGE 51
Dalmatian

PAGE 33
Springer Spaniel

PAGE 38-39
West Highland White
Terrier

PAGE 44
Bassett Hound

PAGE 48
Cockerpoo

PAGES 52-53
Border Collie

PAGES 34-35
Danish-Swedish
Farmdogs

PAGE 40
Black Labrador

PAGE 45
Border Collie

PAGE 49
Siberian Huskies

PAGE 54
Jack Russell Terrier

PAGE 36
American
Staffordshire Terrier

PAGE 41
Catalan Sheepdog

PAGE 46
Springer Spaniel

PAGE 50
American
Staffordshire Terrier

PAGE 55
Golden Retriever

PAGES 56-57
Dachshund

PAGES 62-63
Poodle

PAGE 68
Irish Setter

PAGE 73
Italian Corso Dog

PAGE 79
Poodle

PAGE 83
Dachshund

PAGE 58
Chihuahua

PAGES 64-65
Mixed Breed

PAGE 69
Yorkshire Terrier

PAGES 74-75
Hungarian Vizsla

PAGE 80
American Pit Bull
Terrier

PAGES 84-85
Boston Terrier

PAGE 59
Giant Schnauzer

PAGE 66
Samoyed

PAGES 70-71
Coton de Tulear

PAGES 76-77
Border Collie

PAGE 81
Jack Russell Terrier

PAGE 86
Weimaraner

PAGE 60-61
Tibetan Terrier

PAGE 67
Yorkshire Terrier

PAGE 72
Beagle

PAGE 78
Rhodesian Ridgeback

PAGE 82
Welsh Springer
Spaniel

PAGE 87
Dachshund

PAGES 88-99
Spaniel Cross

PAGE 93
Beagle

PAGE 98
Lhasa Apso

PAGE 103
Afghan Hound

PAGE 107
Newfoundland

PAGES 112-113
Labrador Retriever

PAGE 90
French Bulldog

PAGES 94-95
Schnauzer Cross

PAGE 99
American
Staffordshire Terrier

PAGE 104
Border Terrier

PAGE 108
Jack Russell Terrier

PAGES 114
Bearded Collie

PAGE 91
Yorkshire Terrier

PAGE 96
Cavalier King Charles
Spaniel

PAGES 100-101
Havanese

PAGE 105
Dachshund

PAGE 109
Yorkshire Terrier

PAGE 115
Mixed Breed

PAGE 92
Rough Collie

PAGE 97
German Shepherd

PAGE 102
Poodle

PAGE 106
Bulldog

PAGES 110-111
Papillon

PAGES 116-117
Border Collie

PAGE 118
Jack Russell Terrier

PAGE 123
St. Bernard

PAGE 129
Soft-coated Wheaten
Terrier

PAGE 134
Dobermann

PAGE 138
Border Terrier

PAGE 119
Bergamasco

PAGE 124-125
Maltese

PAGE 130
Miniature Pinscher

PAGE 135
American Staffordshire
Terrier

PAGE 139
Dalmatian and Beagle

PAGES 120-121
Mixed Breed

PAGES 126-127
Springer Spaniel

PAGE 131
Chihuahua

PAGE 136
Dogue de Bordeaux

PAGE 122
Border Collie

PAGE 128
Rottweiler

PAGES 132-133
French Mastiff

PAGE 137
Goldendoodle